ISBN 978-1-5282-2126-9
PIBN 10902814

For support please visit www.forgottenbooks.com

1 MONTH OF
FREE
READING

at

www.ForgottenBooks.com

By purchasing this book you are eligible for one month membership to ForgottenBooks.com, giving you unlimited access to our entire collection of over 1,000,000 titles via our web site and mobile apps.

To claim your free month visit:

www.forgottenbooks.com/free902814

CATALOGUE OF

The Remarkably Fine Collection Of

HARD TIMES TOKENS

FORMED BY

HENRY C. MILLER, ESQR.,

OF NEW YORK CITY.

An Almost Complete Series In The Best Condition Obtainable. By All Means The Finest Collection Of These Tokens Ever Offered At Public Sale.

Also a General Assortment of Coins, Medals, Paper Money, Tokens, Pistols, Weapons and Curiosities, the Properties of Several Individuals, To Be Offered Without Reserve at Public Auction Sale, In One Session,

AT THE ELDER AUCTION ROOMS

32 E. 23rd St., N. Y. City,

ON SATURDAY, MARCH 11, 1916,

At One Thirty O'clock in the Afternoon.

THOMAS L. ELDER, Auctioneer.

———

NOTE.—The Coins, Medals Paper Money, etc., will be on exhibition on date of sale, from 9 to 1.   -:-   -:-   -:-   -:-

Catalogued by

THOMAS L. ELDER, Numismatist

Member, American Numismatic Society, Fellow, Royal Numismatic Society, of Great Britain, Member British Numismatic Society, London, Member of the New York Numismatic Club, Member of the American Numismatic Association, etc.   :-:   -:-   -:-

Thirty-two East Twenty-third St., New York City.

Telephone 5899 Gramercy.   Registered Cable Address "Ranfurly," New York.

IMPORTANT NOTICE.

Note that your bids must be at SO MUCH FOR EACH PIECE.
The bid sheet will be found at end of this catalogue.

SIZES OF COINS AND MEDALS.

in this Catalogue given in Millimetres.

ABBREVIATIONS.

AR.—Silver
AE.—Bronze
Abt.—About.
B.—Brass.
D.—Pence.
Dif.—Different.
F.—Fine.
Fa.—Fair.

G.—Good.
h. c.—Hair-cord.
L.—Left.
Lib.—Liberty.
MM.—Milimeters.
Obv.—Obverse.
Oct.—Octagonal.
Pf.—Proof.

R.—Right.
Rev.—Reverse.
U.—Unc.
Unc.—Uncirculated.
V.—Very.
Var.—Variety.
Var.—Varieties.
W. M.—White Metal.

U. S. Mints are Designated as Follows:

C.—Charlotte.
C. C.—Carson City.
D.—Dahlonega.

O.—New Orleans.
S.—San Francisco.
Without Letter—Philadelphia.

CONDITIONS OF SALE.

This is a bone-fide public sale, for prompt cash settlement, and irresponsible persons who are not sure whether they can pay for what they bid on, are asked not to bid. The cataloguer has taken special pains to describe each lot accurately. Errors will be corrected, but he reserves the sole right to decide upon any claims. These are only conditions under which bids will be received.

Coins and medals are sold at so **much per PIECE**, and no lot will be separated. The auctioneer will accept any bid up to 50c., then 5c up to $2.50, when 10c. advance must be bid, up to $10.00, when no advance under 25 cents will be accepted. If there are 5 pieces in the lot and you wish to pay $5.00 for the entire lot, then bid $1.00.

Auction sales are **strictly for cash.** Parties unknown to me and bidding for the first time, must give bank or other reliable reference, or their bids will not be executed.

Forward your bids as early as possible, as thousands of bids have to be entered. Do not make ridiculously low bids, such as 10c. and 15c. on foreign silver coins worth several times over as bullion. Write your bids plainly, with a pen if practicable.

Where the number of pieces in a lot is not given after the description, there is but one piece in the lot.

Be sure you bid on the lot you wish to buy.

All coins, etc., are genuine unless otherwise described.

My charge for executing bids will be 5 per cent. No charge made for bidding except for lots actually purchased. Remit by money order or New York draft.

Priced catalogue of this sale sent for $1.00 cash in advance.

If any further information is required as to valuation of lots, or how to bid, please write the cataloguer. THOMAS L. ELDER.

THE HENRY C. MILLER COLLECTION OF HARD TIMES TOKENS.

The many collectors who are interested in the Jackson, or Hard Times Tokens will realize after a study of this catalogue that the Miller collection, offers to them an unprecedented opportunity to secure the very choicest and rarest examples obtainable from the finest collection ever offered at public auction sale. The collection is nearly complete, lacking very few numbers. Mr. Miller had no other reason for deciding to sell his collection than that he had almost completed it, and found very few opportunities for adding to it. These tokens, issued by private individuals, and by merchants, during the period of financial stress, cover the interesting times in our political history, the days of Andrew Jackson, Martin Van Buren and William H. Harrison. It is to be hoped that other tokens of the same period, not listed in Mr. Low's valuable work, may be added in the near future, for at the present time the interest in these tokens is keen, and good prices are being realized for rarities and for pieces in special condition. Be sure and favor me with some bids.

Those who are not interested in tokens will find many other items of interest listed herein, in Coins, Paper Money, Medals, Weapons and Curios.

THOMAS L. ELDER.

Cataloguer.

New York, February 14, 1916.

CATALOGUE.

THE COLLECTION OF HARD TIMES TOKENS, FORMED BY

Henry C. Miller, Esq.,

of New York City.

1   Low 1. ANDREW JACKSON. Head to r. Rev. THE BANK MUST PERISH. In wrth, THE UNION MUST AND SHALL BE PRESERVED. Copper. Very fine. Exceedingly rare. Rarity 6.

3   Low 3. Civilian bust to r. Rev. WE COMMEMORATE THE GLORIOUS VICTORIES ETC. Brass. Slight nick on reverse, otherwise very fine. Rare.

4   Low 4. Togated bust of Jackson to r. Rev. Same as preceding. Strong even impression. Uncirculated. Gem piece. Very rare.

5   Low 5. Military bust of Jackson facing. Rev. Eagle in wreath, berries on branch. THE GALLANT & SUCCESSFUL DEFENDER, etc. Brass. Very good. Rare.

6   Low 6. Obv. A ship sailing to l. FOR THE CONSTITUTION HURRA! Rev. FLOURISH COMMERCE, FLOURISH INDUSTRY. etc. Brass. About uncirculated. Choice and very rare.

7   Low 7. Liberty Cap in Glory of rays. THE GLORIOUS WHIG VICTORY of 1834. Rev. Ship. FELLOW CITIZENS, SAVE YOUR CONSTITUTION. Copper. Uncirculated. Brown color. Excessively rare and seldom offered in any condition.

8   Low 8. Boar running to l. Small bust of Jackson. Perfect and cracked dies. Unc. 2 pcs.

9   Low 9. Same as last, but struck in brass. Silvered. Uncirculated. Rare state.

10   Low 10. Same general types, but Jackson has broader shoulders. Sharp uncirculated gem. Uncirculated, partly red. May be best known specimen.

11   Low 11. Same as last, but brass. Silvered as lot 9. Mint state. Rare gem. Finest known specimen. Excessively rare.

12   Low 12. Jackson with sword and Purse. Balking donkey. A PLAIN SYSTEM, etc. Uncirculated. Scarce.

13   Low 13. Bust of Wm. H. Seward to left. Rev. Eagle. A FAITHFUL FRIEND TO OUR COUNTRY Brass Extremely fine and rare.

14   Low 14. Wm. H. Seward. Bust, similar. Rev. Eagle. THE GLORY AND PRIDE OF OUR NATION. Brass Extremely fine. Very rare.

15   Low 15. Wm. H. Seward. Similar obv., but legend differently ar-
      ranged. Rev. Same as 13. A FAITHFUL FRIEND, etc. Brass Very
      fine. Rare.

16   Low 16. Gulian C. Verplanck Bust to left, name. Rev. Eagle. A
      FAITHFUL FRIEND TO OUR COUNTRY. Brass. Nearly bright un-
      circulated. Very rare specimen, one of the best known examples.

17   Low 17. A donkey running to left. Short ground below him. Rev·
      Tortoise, safe. Extremely fine. Excessively rare, especially in this
      choice condition. Steel color.

18   Low 18. Same general types. EXPERIMENT. Unc. Half red.

19   Low 19. Same general types. Unc., red.

20   Low 20. Same general types. FINANCIERING. Unc. Bright red.

21   Low 21. Homely female head to left, stars, date. Rev. NOT ONE
      CENT, etc. Small nick before mouth, Almost· uncirculated. Partly
      red. May be the finest known specimen.

22   Low 22. Ugly head to left, the head smaller than last. NOT ONE
      CENT. etc. Small nick before mouth, Almost uncirculated. Very
      rare gem.

23   Low 23. Female head 1. Largest date in series. Rev. NOT ONE
      CENT, etc. Ex. Fine. Very rare.

24   Low 24. Female head to left, with chaplet of Laurel. Above E PLUR-
      IBUS UNUM. 1837. (smallest date). Rev. NOT ONE CENT, etc.
      Low 24. Copper. Uncirculated, sharp. Excessively rare. R. 7.

25   Low 27. Head to left, with chaplet of laurel leaves, stars below motto,
      and date larger than last. Rev. NOT ONE CENT, etc. a star on each
      side of FOR. Uncirculated, glossy black. Excessively rare. Rarity
      7.

26   Low 28. Head to 1, with plain hair-cord, 6 stars on left. Rev. Wreath
      in which NOT ONE CENT etc. 6 berries outside, 7 inside. Very fine.
      Rare.

27   Low 29. Ugly large, masculine head to 1. NOT ONE CENT, etc, let-
      tering large. Very fine, glossy brown. Rare in any condition.

28   Low 30. Homely head to left, with sharp features, motto, stars, date.
      Rev. NOT ONE CENT, etc. Sharp uncirculated, sharp, glossy color.
      Very choice and rare.

29   1837. Low 31. Lib. head. Rev. similar. Uncirculated, half red.

30   Low 32. Female head. NOT ONE CENT, etc. Unc., sharp, glossy
      brown. Rare.

31   Low 33. Somewhat similar to last. Unc., red.

32   Low 34. Somewhat similar head. Unc. Glossy brown.

33   Low 35. Somewhat similar head. NOT ONE CENT, etc. Sharp, un-
      circulated.

34 Low 36. Similar head, and rev. Unc., red. Rare.

35 Low 37. **Bentonian Currency.** MINT DROP. Unc., red. Rare.

36 Low 38. Liberty head. LBENTONIAN. Unc, some redness. Rare.

37 Low 39. Same obverse MILLIONS FOR DEFENSE. Unc., partly red.

38 Low 40· Head. SPECIÉ PAYMENTS, etc. Unc., red. Rare.

39 Low 41. Obv. wrecked ship, no lightning. Rev. NOT ONE CENT
    FOR TRIBUTE, etc. Attempted puncture through 3 of date 1837.
    otherwise Unc. Copper. Excessively rare. R 7.

40 Low 43. Wrecked ship, with lightning. Rev. NOT ONE CENT, etc.
    Unc. glossy black color. Excessively rare. R 7.

41 Low 44. Jackson in treasure chest. Ship. Unc., brown.

42 Low 45. Phoenix. Rev. NOT ONE CENT. Unc., partly red.

43 Low 46. Phoenix. NOT ONE CENT. Unc, half red.

44 Low 47. Phoenix, MAY TENTH, etc., strings to wreath. Unc., red.

45 Low 48. Phoenix. MAY TENTH. No strings to wrth. Unc. brown,
    Rare.

46 Low 49. HALF CENT WORTH OF PURE COPPER. Unc., traces of
    redness. Very rare condition.
    list. Unc., one bright red. 3 pcs.

47 Low 51. Jackson, chest. Donkey. The three varieties given in Low's
    list. Unc. 1 bright red. 3 pcs.

48 Low 52. Jackson in safe. Donkey. Brass. Briliant uncirculated.
    Rare gem, possibly finest known specimen.

49 Low 53. Jackson in safe. Large head, coat with 8 buttons. Rev.
    Large bodied donkey. Sharp, even impression. Glossy steel color,
    with original red. Gem piece, maybe finest known example.

50 Low 54. Kneeling Slave. AM I NOT A WOMAN, etc., Unc., red. Gem.

51 Low 55. Ugly head. LOCO FOCO. Unc., glossy brown Rare.

52 Low 56. Bust of Van Buren to left. Rev. Safe Copper. Ex. fine, holed,
    as usual, over head. Scarce.

54 Low 58. Ship sailing. Circle of stars, MILLIONS FOR DEFENCE,
    etc. Bright red, uncirculated. Rare gem.

55 Low 59.· Ship. NOT ONE CENT. Share, Unc., red turning to steel.

56 Low 60. Wrecked ship, straight deck, no bowsprit. Unc.
    CY. Extremely fine. Excessive rare. R. 6.

57 Low 61. Wrecked Ship, curved deck, end pointing to E in CURREN-
    CY. Extremely fine. Excessively rare. R. 6.

58 Low 62. Ship sailing. Wrecked ship. Sharp unc., partly red.

59 Low 63. Ship. WEBSTER CREDIT. Rev. Wrecked ship, no light-
    ning Unc., red.

60 Low 64. Ship, WEBSTER. CREDIT CURRENCY. Rev. Wrecked
    ship. Unc., traces of redness.

61 Low 65. Ship. Leaf before and after WEBSTER, instead of star. Rev. Head of Low 30. Unc., partly red. Rare, especially so choice.

62 Low 66. A steer. Ship. AGRICULTURE AND COMMERCE. Unc. steel color. Rare.

63 Low 67. Head 1. Roses and leaves. E PLURIBUS UNUM. Rev. SPECIE PAYMENTS, etc. Unc., partly red.

64 Low 68. Head, date 1841. Rev. MINT DROP. Unc., brown.

65 Low 69. Head, date 1841. Rev. NOT ONE CENT, Roses and leaves. Unc., red. Choice.

66 Low 70. Head. Roses and leaves. Rev. NOT ONE CENT. 3 berries outside, 4 inside, large berries, small letters. Unc., sharp. Ex. Rare. Rarity 7.

67 Low 71. Head, 1. Roses and leaves, date 1841. Rev. NOT ONE CENT, etc. 6 pointed star on each side of FOR. Ex. fine. Excessively rare. R. 7.

68 Low 72. Francis L. Brigham, New Bedford. Die-break on obv. Fine to very fine. Rarity 4. Has high auction record.

69 Low 72. Same token. Struck over Jackson In Safe Token of 1837. Very fine. Excessively rare. First of this sort offered for sale.

70 Low 73. Francis L. Brigham. View of building. Uncirculated, sharp, glossy piece, steel color. Very rare. Rarity 5.

71 Low 74. Hathaway. Fire-grate. Unc., brown color.

72 Low 75. American Institute. V. Fine.

73 Low 76. American Institute. Unc., partly red.

74 Low 77. Bucklins. BUCKLINS BOOK KEEPING SIMPLIFIED etc. Inscription only both sides. Extremely fine. May be the best known example. Excessively rare.

75 Low 78. Handy. Eagle. Very fine. Scarce.

76 Low 79. Lafayette. Haskins. Fine Rare.

77 Low 79. Lafayette. Duplicate. Good. Scarce.

78 Low 80. W. P. Haskins. Rev. Planing machine. Sharp, uncirculated. Very choice.

79 Low 81. Howell Works Garden. Signum, 1834. Small sized token. Copper. Fine. Rare.

30 Low 83. H. M. & E. I. Richards, Attleboro, Mass. 1834. Lafayette standing. Uncirculated, half red. Rare state.

81 Low 84. S. B. Schenck, Attleboro, Mass. Planing machine V. Fine.

82 Low 86. Lafayette standing. S. L. Wilkins. Fine, glossy brown.

84 Low 88. Ugly female head. Rev. Bucklins Interest Tables. Very fair for this excessively rare piece.

85 Low 89. Ugly head to right. Rev. BUCKLINS INTEREST TABLES. Very good. Excessively rare.

86 Low 92. Bucklins. Inscription both sides. Very fine. Scarce condition. Slight edge defect.

87 Low 93. Bucklins. Rev. Large stars instead of leaves. About uncirculated. May be finest known example of this very rare variety.

88 Low 94. Lafayette standing. Clark & Anthony. About Unc., brown color.

89 Low 95. Merchants Exchange. NOT ONE CENT, etc. Dash. Unc., glossy brown.

90 Low 96. Merchants Exchange. Rarity with dash under CENT and berry opposite second E in DEFENCE. Dented, otherwise good. Excessively rare. Rarity 7. Rated as one of the rarest of all Jackson tokens, and has not been offered for sale for many years.

91 Low 97. Merchants Exchange. No dash. Unc, partly red.

92 Low 98. Merchants Exchange. Rev. N. Y. Joint Stock Exch. Unc., red, choice.

93 Low 99. Plow. Walsh. SPEED THE PLOW, etc. Fine, scarce.

94 Low 100. Lafayette. Walsh, LANSINGBURGH. About Unc., scarce.

95 101. Lafayette. Walsh, LANSINBURG. Unc., red. Rare state.

96 Low 103. R. & W. Robinson. Fine.

97 Low 104. American Institute Obv. Rev. R. & W. Robinson. Brilliant uncirculated. Rare gem.

98 Low 105. American Institute Obv. Hyphen between New and York. Fine. Very rare.

99 Low 106. Walton, Walker & Co., New Orleans, 1836 large brass token. Has a large dent, otherwise uncirculated. Excessively rare and seldom offered in any condition.

100 A boot. Hanry Anderson. Very fine.

101 Low 108. Obv. a flower on a pedestal. R. L. Baker, Charleston, S. C. 1837. Feuchtwanger metal. Sharp uncirculated. Finest known and should bring a very large price. Rarity 7.

102 Low 109. Benedict & Burnham card. An eagle. Ex. fine. Rare.

103 Low 110. Head. Centre Market. Sharp, uncirculated, glossy brown.

104 Low 111. Head. Centre Market 14th Ward, New York Unc., red.

105 Low 112. Head of Low 29. H. Crossman. Unc. Head partly weak as usual. Rare.

106 Low 113. Eagle. Crossman card. Sharp unc., red Gem piece.

107 Low 114. Head of Low 28. Dayton card. Unc., partly red. Very choice and rare.

108 Low 115. DeVeau; Chatham Square, New York. Uncirculated, red. Very rare state, as fine as any.

109 Low 116. Maverick Coach, 1837. Feuchtwanger metal. Ex. fine. V. Rare.

110 Low 117. Arms of N. Y. Feuchtwanger's Three Cents. Uncirculated. Scarce.

111 Low 118. Eagle standing on a rock, 1837. Feuchtwanger's Three Cents. Extremely fine. Exceedingly rare. With a record of $100 for an uncirculated specimen. (Note. I bought the token).

112 Low 119. Eagle, smaller than on last token, standing on a rock, 1837 Feuchtwanger. Three Cents Almost uncirculated. Excessively rare, more so than Low 118.

113 Low 120. Defiant eagle to right, 1837. ONE CENT . etc. Feuchtwanger metal. Four different dies. Ex. F. and Uncirculated. 4 pcs.

114 Low 122. Liberty head. Jarvis token. Uncirculated, red. Very choice and rare.

115 Low 123. Female head as on Low 30. Jarvis token. Sharp, uncirculated, partly red. May be finest known specimen. Perfection.

116 Low 124. Nath'l. March Simes. Very fine.

117 Low 125. Ugly head, as on Low 29. Maycock card Uncirculated. Very rare thus.

118 Low 126. Eagle with open wings. Maycock card. About Uncirculated.

119 Low 127. Scissors, comb. Phalons Hair Cutting. Bright red. Very rare.

120 Low 127. Phalons. Duplicate. Extremely fine, some redness. Rare.

121 Low 128. Eagle, 1837. R. E. Russel, "I. O. U. 12½c?" Feuchtwanger metal Fine. Excessively rare. Rarity 7.

122 Low 129. Roxbury Coaches. Feuchtwanger Metal. Almost uncirculated. Rare. Obv. A.

123 Low 130. Phoenix. J. M. L. & W. H. Scoville. Unc, bright red. May be finest known. Very rare.

124 Low 131. A. C. Smith, Haselton & Palmer. About fine. Rare.

125 Low 132. E. F. Sise & Co., Ex. fine.

126 Low 133. A clock face. Smiths. Hour hand touches right side of "X," minute hand points between 2nd and 3rd dots. Sharp, uncirculated. Very rare so choice.

127 Low 134. Smiths. "Establishment" straight, hour hand points to center of "X," minute hand between 1st and 2nd dots. Fine. Very rare.

128 Low 135. Smiths. "Establishment" curved upwards. Hour hand points to right of "X," minute hand between 2nd and 3rd dots. Unc., bright red. Very rare.

129 Low 136. Smith's. Small ornaments beside "7½", "Establishment" curved up. Uncirculated. Rare.

130 Low 138. Smith's. The ornaments larger than on last. Sharp uncirculated, Very rare in this state.

131 Low 139. S. S. B., above two leaves, date '1837'' Very large. Rev.
Cross form of four leaves, and border of heavy leaf ornaments. Un.
circulated, glossy black, but possibly brass. Exceedingly rare, in same
class with Low 149, and just as valuable.

132 Low 140. Liberty head, stars. Erza B. Sweet. Small, thin flan.
Slightest edge nick. Uncirculated, glossy brown. Very rare.

133 Low 141. Liberty head. Sweet card. Large flan. Fine. Rarity 4.

134 Low 142. An Eagle Bergen Iron Works. Stars dividing lettering.
Brass. Sharp uncirculated, bright. May be finest known specimen.

135 Low 140. Liberty head, stars. Ezra B. Sweet. Small, thin flan.
stars divide lettering. Very small die break. Copper. Small flan.
Uncirculated, glossy black. Rare.

136 Low 143. Eagle. Bergen Card. Same as last, but on larger planchet.
Copper. Fine. Rare.

137 Low 145. Liberty head to left, large stars. Bucklins Book-keeping.
Small flan. Uncirculated. Very rare.

138 Low 145. Same token, larger flan. About uncirculated. Very rare.

139 Low 146. Similar head to right. The rare card of Carpenter &
Mosher. DRY GOODS in wreath. Uncirculated. Finest known specimen, Soldom offered in any condition. Should bring a big price.

140 Low 148. Boquet. Duseaman card. V. Fine.

142 Low 150. J. Gibbs. "MEDALS AND TOKENS." Fine. Exceedingly
rare, with a recent high auction record.

143 Low 151. Steer. Rev. A boquet. W. Gibbs token. Fine to very fine.
Ex. Rare.

144 Low 153. Abraham Riker. Shoe-Dealer. 3 berries outside, 5 inside,
no dash below "Cent." Unc. Red. Rare.

145 Low 154. Riker. 2 berries outside, 6 inside. Dash under CENT.
Fine. Very rare.

146 Low 155. Steer. Rev. Boquet. T. D. Seaman. Uncirculated, brown
color. Excessively rare.

147 Low 156. Rude head to right, with TROY on coronet. Rev. Screw-
bolt MACHINE SHOP, etc. Very good. Excessively rare.

148 Low 158. Loomis Card. An eagle standing on arrows to right, holding three large links in its beak, the links falling over its body. A
LOOMIS CLEVELAND OIHO (Sic!). Rev. DEALER IN GROCERIES,
LIQUORS, WINES & C. No. 34 MERWIN ST. 1843." below, a serpent.
Thick flan. Small edge nicks. Fine. Extremely rare. Only 2 or 3
known. This and the two tokens following were used by Mr. Low in
the compilation of his well known work on the Jackson Tokens.

149 1843. Loomis Card. An Eagle to right, standing on two arrows wide⁻ ly separated from each other, and holding three very small links in its beak, the links do not touch the body, and are held high above the bird's left wing. A LOOMIS CLEVELAND OIHO (Sic!) Rev. similar to last. A few scratches. Very good. Exceedingly rare. Mr. Miller knows of no other.

150 Low 160. A. Loomis. Eagle to left, without links in its beak. A LOOMIS (part illegible because struck over another token) CLEVE-LAND. OIHO (Sic!) Rev. DEALER IN GROCERIES, LIQUORS WINES & C. No. 34 Merwin St. 1843.''. Small hole over eagle's head. Fine for the crude piece. Believed to be unique.

Note.—The three above tokens will be offered as one set.

151 Low 162. Bust of Van Buren to right, name, stars, sprig. Rev. Eagle "INDEPENDENT TREASURY JULY 4, 1840." Copper. Fine. Holed, as issued. Very rare.

152 Low 163. A large rose. Howell Works Garden. TOKEN. Fine. Rare.

153 Low 164. Planing Machine. Richards. Schenck. Very fine. Rare.

154 Low 171. Jackson in chest. Similar to Low 51, but gilded before strik-ing. Unc. full gilt. Ex. Rare.

155 Low 172. Bust of Van Buren to left. Safe. SOBER SECOND THOUGHTS. etc. Brass, Holed, as usual. Very fine. Rare in this metal.

158 Low 181. Obv. A star, in which an eagle. Between its points C-W-B-18-43 the 4 retrograde. Rev. Blank. Feuchtwanger metal. V. Fine. Very rare.

159 Low 182. C. W. B. As last, but SILVER. Very fine, and much rarer than preceding.

Hard Times Tokens, Not In Low's List, Etc.

161 ONE CENT within wreath, with 13 berries. Rev. Same design, but different die, and 15 berries in wreath. Size 22. Feuchtwanger metal. I have never catalogued it. V. Fine. Ex. Rare. If in the list would be a $75 or $100 piece.

162 1840. Bust of M. Van Buren to left. Name, etc. Rev. Unbalanced scales. WEIGHED IN THE BALANCE, etc. Brass. Holed. Unc.

163 Bust of Andrew Jackson to left, Name. Rev. THE NATION'S GOOD. in wreath in which 7 berries and 8 acorns. Brass. VG. Holed. Rare.

164 Bust of Jackson facing. Name. Rev. HERO OF NEW ORLEANS. in wrth of laurel in which 20 berries. Brass. Holed at top. V. Fine.

164a Bust of Andrew Jackson to 1. Name. Rev. "The Nation's Pride," in wreath of 7 berries and 4 acorns, without stars. Brass. Very fine. Very rare.

165 Head of Van Buren, similar to lot 162. Rev. A flag-pole. DEMO-CRATS! TO THE POLLS AND VICTORY WILL BE OURS. Fine. Excessively rare, possibly the rarest of all Van Buren tokens. Brass.

166 1860. **Various tokens.** Lincoln's campaign. NOT ONE CENT FOR SLAVERY, etc. Eagle. V. Fine.

167 1860. Bust of Lincoln to right. Rev. Rail-splitting scene. Brass. Unc.

168 Stephen A. Douglas. Bust to left, by S. P. Dates of birth and death. Rev. "Douglas Monume————nt (Sic !) Association, Cornerstone LAID September 6, 1866.". WM. Size 35. With this error possibly unique. Unc.

MISCELLANEOUS LOT OF COINS.

169 **Small U. S. Cts.** 1868-73, Unc. '94-5-6-.Brill Proofs. 5 pcs.

170 Connecticut Cents. Varieties G & V. G. 10 pcs.

171 (A. D. 1149). **Foreign Coppers. Ortokides** Coppers. Amid and Keifa Fachr-Eddin Kara Arslon. Bust to left. Inscr. Thomsen 925. Fine; rare.

172 (1149). Same ruler. Bust front face. Inscr. Thomsen 927 VG.

173 (1152). Nedschm-Eddin-Albi. Two heads. Rev. Head in circle Thomsen. 907 A. Fine. Rare.

174 (1152). Same ruler. Two heads facing. Two figures standing. Remarkably fine specimen, best I have seen. Rare.

175 (1152). Same ruler. Bust to r, similar style to Syrian tetradrachms. Inscr VG. Thomsen 906. Fine. Rare.

176 (1184). Husam Eddin Juluk Arslon. Three figures, one seated with reclining head. Inscription. V.G. Rare. Thomsen 911.

177 (1184). Same ruler. Large bust front face. Rev. Inscription. Very fine and rare example. Thomsen 910.

178 (1233). Mosul (Zeukides of). Bedr-Eddin Lulu. Head to r in square. Inscription. Fine. Rare. Thomsen 936.

179 England, Canada, India, etc. Misc. copper coins and tokens. Many fine. 74 pcs.

180 1752. England. Geo. II. Half Penny. Very fine.

181 Malta, Malay Peninsula, Ionian Islands, Mysore, Krisna Rajah, XX Cash. Fine. Scarce. 6 pcs.

182 St. Helena, Solomon D. & T. Half P. Wm. Till 1834 ¼ D; Bladud, Northampton and Anti-Tax farthings. Fine, choice. 5 pcs.

183 Ionian Islands. 10 Oboli, 1819. Brilliant proof. Excessively rare. First I have noticed.

184 St. Helena. Lions, shields, Half Penny 1821, Unc; Solomon, Dickson & Taylor. V. F. 2 pcs.

185 Antwerp. Napoleon Siege 5 and 10 C. Unc., red. Rare state. 2 pcs.

186 Siege of Antwerp. Louis XVIII. 10c, Unc., red, 5c. Fine. 2 pcs.

187 England and Ireland. ½ D. of Geo. II and III (6); Various farthings, Geo. II to Edw. VII. fine to Unc. 14 pcs.

188 1783. Gibraltar. Blockade penny or medal. Sea battle. Rev. Sinking of the Royal George. "ROYAL GEORGE ADMIRAL KEMPENFELT, 1783.". V. Fine. Ex. Rare. First in my sales.

189 Gibraltar. Robert Keeling & Sons. 1 & 2 Quartos. View of the rock. V. F. latter Uncirculated. V. Rare. 2 pcs.

190 1810. Gibraltar. Robt. Keeling. Lion, key 1 & 2 Quartos. 3 diff. VF. to Unc. 3 pcs.

191 Gibraltar. R. Cattons, James Spittles, 1 & 2 Quartos; Victoria. 2 and ½ Quartos G. to V. F. 6 pcs.

192 West Indies. Curacoa. 3 In Circle, Cstps on triangular section of Spanish 8 Reals silver. 3 Reals. Wood, p. 24, Figure 101. Fine.

193 Tobago. Billon Sou. Cstpd. TB. Wood p. 20, figure 80. Fine.

194 1809. Tyrol. Andreas Hofer, The man who defied Napoleon. Arms. 1 Kreuzer. VF. Rare.

195 1809. Tyrol. Andreas Hofer. 20 Kreuzers. Arms. Uncirculated, bright. Rare state.

196 **Ancient Roman Small Bronze.** Victorinus, Probus & others to Constantius II, including City of Rome, with Wolf, twins. Many fine. 16 pcs.

Lot of Fine Italian & Other Crowns, Etc.

Very Scarce On Account Of The War

197 1592. Strasburg (Germany). Rare Klippe thaler, uniface style. Three shields, dividing date "15-92"; below them "80·" Fine and Excessively rare. See Mailliet. First in my sales. Valuable.

198 1605. Tuscany. Half-length bust of Ferdinand I, in armour holding sceptre, name, titles, date. Rev. Crowned arms. PISA INVETUSTAE MAIESTATIS MEMORIAM. Fine. Rare.

199 1642. Tuscany. Unusual ruffed bust of Ferdinand II. Name, titles, beneath the bust the date, with figure 2 reversed, (retrograde). Rev. St. John the Baptist, name. Date beneath, correct 1642. Broad crown. Fine. Remarkable as having a date on either side, the one on obv. being in error. Very rare.

200 (1552-80) Hohenstein. St. Andrew standing. Arms of Wolfgang. Thaler. Fine. and Rare. Value $7.00.

201 1796. Neapolitan Republic. Liberty standing. Seventh year of Liberty. CARLINI DODICI. Crown. Fine. Rare.

202 1617. Erfurt, Germany. Arms. Two wild men supporting shield with wheel; above them a wheel MON ARGENTEA CIVITATIS ERFORDI. Rev. Arms in shield DATE CAESARIS CAESARI QUAE DEI DEO. Broad crown. Fine. Very rare. First in my sales.

203 1699. Henneberg—Ilmenau. Satirical scene. Two men holding Marionette figure, etc. Arms. NACH DEM ALTEN REICHS SCHRO-TUND KORN 1699.". Good. Very rare, first in my sales.

204 1650. Gotha. Peace Thaler Ernest Der Fromme. Peace of Westphalia. Uncirculated. Very rare.

205 1591. Brunswick. Henry Julius. Truth Thaler. Christ, surrounded by shields, etc. Rev. POST EPIS HALD B. E. L. P. C. HENRI IULI. DEI GRATIA." RECTE FACIENDO NEMINEM TIMEAS 1597." About fine. Very rare.

206 1643. Metz, St. Stephen, with halo. Arms. Broad thaler. Very fine Rare.

207 1815. Sardinia. Bust of Victor Emanuel (Contemporary with Napoleon.) with hair tied in knot. Eagle Soldi 2.6. Billon. Uncirculated, bright. Very rare state.

208 1809.. Westphalia. Bust of Jerome Napoleon Bonaparte. Rev. value, ⅔ thaler. Uncirculated. Very rare.

209 Mozambique. Oblong Counterstamped Onza, or dollar. About fine. Rare.

210 China. Large head of present Emperor (or prest). Yuan Shi Kai, in military dress. Chinese in wrth. Brilliant mint state dollar. Scarce.

Rare or Scarce Jackson Tokens, Etc.

211 Low 7. The Glorious Whig Victory. Radiate cap. Ship sailing. Good to very good, several light edge dents. Excessively rare. If perfect worth $60.00. Second time in my sales.

212 Low 53. Thick donkey. About fine. Scarce.

213 Low 56. Van Buren. Rev. Safe. Copper, with traces of silvering. Ex. fine. Scarce. Holed, as usual.

214 Low 144. Bergen Iron Wks. Circles. Abt. fine. Die about perfect.

215 Low 115. Deveau. Boot. Abt. fine, scarce.

216 Daniel Webster. Bust to right, name, dates birth, death. Webster Statue unveiling, Concord, NH. WM. Size 40. Unc. V. Rare.

217 Obv. A nude woman seated by a bath. "Beck's Public Baths." Bronze, old cent size. About fine. Rare.

Rare U. S. Pattern Coins.

218   1881. .**Three Cents.** Liberty head to left, as on 1883 Nickel Five Cts. Rev. "III" in wreath. Copper proof. Plain edge. Exceedingly rare. A-W. No. 1652. Rarity 8.

219   1881. Cent. Same type head, thicker flan. Rev. "1" in wrth. Plain edge. Brilliant copper proof. A-W 1655 Excessively rare.

RARE QUARTER EAGLE OF 1796.

219a 1796. Quarter Eagle. Liberty head. Stars. Rev. Heraldic eagle. Very fine, but has a long scratch extending across obverse. Rare and in great demand.

Rare U. S. Gold Three and One Dollars.

220   Three Dollars. 1867. Small nick, otherwise very fine. Very rare. Records to $16.50. Coinage V. small.

221   —As last, date 1870. Ex. fine. V. Rare. Coinage small.

222   —As last, date 1872 Ex. fine. Rare, coinage, small.

223   —1886. Ex. fine, coinage small. Rare.

224   Gold Dollars. 1849. Open wreath. Uncirculated, scarce.

225   —1858. Fine, scarce date.

226   —1878. Ex. fine. Rare.

227   —1882. Ex. fine. Rare, coinage small.

228   1915. Cuba. Dollar. Bust of the President. Arms. Unc. Rare, coinage only about 6,000 and all gone. First offered.

229   **For'n Silver.** 1783. France. Youthful bust of Louis XVI. Arms. Ecu. V. G.

230   1822. France. Bust of Louis XVIII. Arms. 5 Francs. V. Fine.

231   1804 Mexico. Bust of Charles IV. Arms. A GENUINE AMERICAN 1804 DOLLAR!

232   Austria. Franz Jos. and Empress marriage thaler. Fine.

233   1897. Dominica. Head of Liberty by Victory D. Brenner, of N. Y. City. Arms. 1 Peso. Very good.

234   1818. Wurtemburg. Large head of William. Rev. Value Broad Kronenthaler. Fine Scarce type.

235   1626. Nuremburg. Arms of H. R. Empire. Thaler. Good.

LARGE LOTS OF OLD U. S. CENTS.

235a Duplicate Large U. S. Cents, before 1815. None holed. Avg. Fair. 50 pcs.

235b Large U. S. Cents.   Duplicates, but a large assortment of dates, Good
      and very good. 250 pcs.
235c Large U. S. Cents.   Large assortment of dates. G. and V. G. 250 pcs.
235d Large U. S. Cents.   Good to very good, with many different dates. 250
      pcs.
235e Large U. S. Cents.   Good. Many dates. 200 pcs.

Foreign Silver Crowns.

236   1780. Courland, Captured by Germany in this War). Bust of Peter.
      Rev. Arms. Handsome groad crown in mint state. V. Rare.
237   1784. Palatinate. Large head of Carl. Theodore. Arms, crowned.
      Broad Conventions thaler. Fine.
238   Augsburg. Bust of Francis I. ofAustria. and H. R. Empire. Rev.
      Arms. Thaler. Small dent. V. Fine.
239   1765. Birkenfels. Bust of Christian IV. Arms. Thaler. Good. Rare.
240   1811. France. Bust of Napoleon Bonaparte. 5 Fcs. Bordeau Mint.
      Unc.
241   1811. Italy. Napoleon as King. Bust. 5 Lire. Abt. Fine.
242   1813. Sicily & Naples. Bust of James Napoleon, with flowing hair.
      Arms. 5 Lire. Abt. Fine. Scarce.
243   1795. Schleswig-Holstein. Species thaler. Good.
244   Basel. Shields in circle, shooter. 5 Fcs. V. Fine.

Encased Postage Stamps.

245   1c Joseph L. Bates, Boston. Very good. Rare.
246   10c. Gage Brothers & Drake. Ex. fine, choice and rare.
247   1c Schapker & Bussing, Evansville, Ind. Very good. Excessively rare.
248   10c. Schapker & Bussing, Evansville, Ind. V. Fine. Excessively rare
      and valuable.
249   24 Cts. J. F. Gault. Ex. fine. Excessively rare.

Rare Small Cent of 1856.

250   1856. Cent, with flying eagle. Uncirculated. Rare. In great de-
      mand.

American Colonial and Continental Coins.

251   **Penn'a Bungstowns.** Charles Fox MP. Bust. Harp. North Wales,
      1761. Well executed, and practically Unc. Rare. Atkins 32.
252   Alfred. Bearded head r. Hibernia seated, her before her. BRITONS
      GLORY. Ex. Fine, glossy brown. Atkins No. 2.

253 Clauduis Romanus. Delectat Rus. 1774. Fine. Atkins. 55·

254 Clauduis Romanus. Delectat Rus. 1771. A. 41. Ex. F. Some red-ness.

255 Clauduis Romanus Britannias Isle, 1774. Atkins 48. VF. Some red-ness.

256 George Gordon Britons Rule. 1772. Atkins 120. Abt. Fine.

257 George Gordon. Head L. Britons Rule, 1791. Brittania to left. Very fine. V. Rare. Not in Atkins.

258 George Rules. Harp, North Wales, 1781. Stops both sides. Fine. Not in Atkins. Rare.

259 George Rules Britannia Isles. VG. A 159.

260 George Rules. I. G. Rev. Britain's Isles, 1730. With I. G. not in At-kins. VG.

261 George Rules. No stops. Rev. Harp, North Wales, 1760. A 173. Fine, some redness.

262 George Rules. I. G. Britain's Isles. 1721 Atkins 155. V. G.

263 George Rules. I. G. Britain's Isles. 1721. A different die from last, V. Fair. V. Rare.

264 George Sussex. Gloriovs Iervis. two revs. of last. Fair to Good. 3 pcs.

265 George Rules. Britains Isles. 1730. Ex. fine. Rare.

266 Counterfeit English Half Pence of Geo. II and III. 14 pcs.

267 NJ. Fugio, Mass., G. & V. G. 5 pcs.

268 Florida. 1/24 Part of a real. Jas. II. Pewter. Fine.

269 1783. Nova Constellatio. Blocked rays. U. S. Cent. Fine.

270 Old Military Buttons 1812 War & later to Civil War, all diff. and scarce. 15 pcs.

VERY RARE HALIFAX TOKEN.

270a HALIFAX. POUND TOKEN. Obv. farm scene, a man plowing, behind him houses trees, etc. HALIFAX INDUSTRIAL SOCIETY LIMITED. Rev. in circle ONE POUND. Around the border. HALI-FAX INDUSTRIAL SOCIETY. LIMITED. Copper. Half penny size. Several dents. Very good. Looks to be period 1840-1860· Unlisted in either Leroux, Breton or Courteau. Who has seen or heard of it?

RARE WELLINGTON SILVER TOKEN

270b Head of Wellington to left. "THE DUKE OF WELLINGTON." Rev. IN ARMS INVINCIBLE IN COUNCIL TRUE in 4 lines; inside wreath of Laurel, etc. Silver, size 19. Ex. Fine. Has been gold plated. Not listed.

PAPER MONEY.

U. S. Fractional Currency

271 **1st Issue.** 5c. Cut edges, No ABNCo. Unc. Rare.

272 10c, 25c, ABNCo. Ex. F. & Unc. 2 pcs.

273 50c. ABNCo. About Unc. 2 pcs.

274 10c ABNCo. Unsevered pair Unc. 2 pcs.

275 **2nd Issue.** 5c Black only, on heavy paper, marked SPECIMEN Cancelled. Unc.

276 25c Silk Fibre Paper. About Unc. Rare.

277 25c. Hardpaper. Gilt letters. Unc.

278 50c. Maroon. Unc.

279 10c. No gilt letters. Unsevered pair. VF. 2 pcs.

280 **Third Issue.** 10c. Washn. Specimens, front and back separate, Autog. sigs. Colby & Spinner. Perfect. 1 lot.

281 50c Justice, front only. Perfect. Specimen.

282 50c Justice. Red back. Fine. Rare.

283 50c Spinner 2 Var. Fine and VF. 2 pcs.

284 50c. Heavy fibre paper, Justice. Unc. Rare.

285 25c Fessenden. Heavy fibre paper. Ex. F. Rare.

286 **4th Issue.** 15c Blue end. Unc. Rare.

287 **Various.** 5c notes (2), 3c (2), 10c notes (11). Mostly good. 15 pcs.

288 5th Issue. 10c, Green seal., VF. 4th, 15c. F. & G. 2 pcs.

289 25c notes, 2nd issue (2), 5th (2) VG. & Unc. 4 pcs.

289a 15c. 4th Issue. 3c 3rd. G. to F. 2 pcs.

MORMON FIVE DOLLARS GOLD.

289b 1849. $5.00. EYE. MITRE. TO THE LORD HOLINESS. Rev. Clasped hands. G. S. L. C. P. G. FIVE DOLLARS. Small dent either side, otherwise Fine. Rare and in great demand.

U. S. GREENBACK CURRENCY.

290 1887. $2. Jefferson. Large seal at r, small at left. Sigs. Allison & Gilfillan. Letter A. Unc.

291 291 1880. $2. Jefferson. Large purplish brown seal at r. Sigs. Bruce & Wyman. Letter C. Unc.

292 1880. $2. Jefferson. As last. Letter D. Unc.

293 1878. $1. Washn. Large oblong seal at r, another small round seal at left. Sigs. Allison & Gilfillan. Letter C. Unc.

294 1878. $1. As last. Letter D. Unc.

295 1880. $1. Washu. Large purplish brown seal at r. Sigs. Bruce & Wyman. VF. Letter D.

296 1891. $1. Stanton. Small red seal at right, open back. Sigs. Tillman & Morgan. Letter E. Unc.

297 1891. $2.00. McPherson. Small red seal at r. Open back. Sigs. Bruce & Roberts. Letter A. Unc. Rare.

298 Rare Sheet of Continental Money. Sept. 26, 1778. Sheet of $5, $7, $8, $20, $30, $40, $50, $60. Unsevered block. Very fine. Ex. Rare. 8 pcs.

299 1776. Conn. Notes for 9 pence, shilling and 40 Shill. Ex. F. cut canceled, none missing; Rare. 3 pcs.

299a 1774. Md. $4.; 1779. S. Car. $70, $90. G. to Fine. 3 pcs.

299b Lot of Foreign Paper Money, including a strip of Cuban 10c notes. Some fine and scarce., mostly diff. 24 pcs.

299c 1777. Georgia. Continental. $7. Seal a hand. Fine. Very rare.

299d 1777. Georgia. Continental. $⅓. Checkered seal. Very good. Very rare. Note 116!

299e 1866. Mormon Great Salt Lake City Corporation note for 25 cts. "Payable in U. S. Currency.". Fine. Rare.

MILITARY AND OTHER MEDALS, WAR TOKENS, ETC.

300 U. S. Army Buttons. Regimental badges, etc. Diff. 18 pcs.

301 U. S. Army Corps enameled badges includes 1st and 3rd Corps. Diff. Very fine. 5 pcs.

302 1687. Battles of Coblenz and Philipsburg. Battle scene. Uniface large bronzed medal. Fine.

303 1790. French Revolution. Soldiers swearing. Rev. 5 Sols. By Monneron. V. Fine.

304 1790. France. Allegorical scene, France before tablet on which A LA PATRIAE, A Paris Le 14 Juillet 1790. Rev. CONFEDERATION DES FRANCOIS. Silver. original.

305 U. S. A. 1846 Mexican War. Arms of NY State. Large silver medal to NY. Soldier. Mexican Battles. Size 53. Fine. Holed near top. Rare.

306 James Buchanan. Large bust front. Rev. Eagle Radiation, names of states. WM. Size 60 V. G.

307 New Haven, Ct. Settlement founding scene. Large WM; Millard Fillmore. Bust. The Union. Lee Statue, New Orleans. WM. 30 to 60 MM. 3 pcs.

308 Millard Fillmore. Bust. The Union. WM. Size 35. VF. Rare.

309 Washington Allston. Large bust to r. Art crowning him. Pewter trial, no lettering. VG. Unique. Size 44.

310   Haverford College, Pa. AE'; Ferd. Latrobe, Mayor Balto. AE. Unc.   2
      pcs.

311   Fred'k. Schiller. Centenary. Germany, NY 1759. WM. VF.

312   **Civil War Tokens.** Kentucky. Thick token, Garrett Townsend. A
      hand, mug. 5c. Unc. V. Rare.

313   —1863. City of NY. Cent. Indian head. ONE CENT. Large F.

314   The Federal Union It Must and Shall **BY** preserved." Fine. Rare error.

315   Ohio. Various cards. Dups. Mostly F. 12 pcs.

316   Various Western War Cards. Most F. Includes Ky. 19 pcs.

317   War Tokens with busts of Washington, Jackson and McClellan, in-
      cludes 1 of Washn. in silver. Fine. Mostly F. 30 pcs.

318   Other Melville, Peace Maker (several), Freaks, uniface, off flans, New
      England, etc. Some scarce. 25 pcs.

319   Various War Tokens, cards and mottoes. Mostly F. 80 pcs.

320   Another lot of War Tokens, all kinds. Mostly Fine. 90 pcs.

321   A third lot of war Tokens, mostly fine. 90 pcs.

322   Civil War Tokens, various mottoes and cards. Mostly F. 90 pcs.

323   Another lot of Civil War Tokens. Mostly Fine. 90 pcs.

324   Another lot of Civil War Tokens, mostly fine. 90 pcs.

325   Large Lot of the lot of Civil War Tokens, various designs, mottoes,
      cards, etc. Mostly Fine. 216 pcs.

326   Lot of Civil War Tokens, mottoes, cards, etc., from all quarters. Most-
      ly fine. 104 pcs.

327   Another lot of War Tokens, from all quarters. Mostly fine. 90 pcs.

328   Benton Sutlers check for 25 cts; Gen. Z. Taylor. Bust. Rev. Lib. std.,
      Lincoln. Bust, silver, with bust. 3 pcs.

329   Jackson Tokens, various, some fine. 21 pcs.

330   NY Medal showing Bartholdi Statue, Liberty Enlightening the World.
      In remembrance of the old friendship, etc. "Both" spelled "Booth."
      AE. Size 50. Unc.

331   Copy of the Greek Dekadrachm of Syracuse. Head. Chariot.

332   Indianapolis 1873-74 Cincinnati Expos 1873; Fairmount, Ohio Church
      medal. Louisville Expo. Scarce. WM. Unc. 6 pcs.

333   France. Henry Giffrard Balloon Ascension. Large AE. with ring View
      of ascension. Fine.

334   Canada. Victoria Bridge Medal. View. Arms, bust. Large WM. Pf.
      WM. Size 60 MM. Fine.

335   1759. Spain. Bust of Isabel II to left by Massonet African War Medal.
      WM. Size 60 MM. Fine.

336   Small Foreign silver medals 10 to 20 MM. Various events, Wm. I **of**
      Prussia, Francis I. Luther, etc. some of ducat size, and some in gold.
      G. to **VF. 9 pcs.**

337   1797. Capitulation of Mantua. Head of Virgilius. Rev. Turretted
      crown. Swan. AE. Size 35. Unc.

338   1816. Milan. Euterpe Musical Society. AE Size 44. Unc.

339   Cardinal Cornelius. Handsome bust to right, name. Rev. Homage.
      AE. Size 46. Unc. Rare.

340   Holland. Brothers Dewitt. Busts of the Grand Pensioners. Inscription.
      V. Loon P. III L. I. 81. Silver. Size 50. Fine.

341   1744. Namur. Handsome youthful bust of Maria Theresa Arms.
      AE. Size. Unc. Rare.

342   1792. Namur. Bust of Francis II. Arms. Coronation. AE. 31. Unc.
      red.

343   France. Louis XIII. Youthful bust to left, in large ruff. Rev. Events
      of reign. Large AE. Size 51 Unc. Choice.

344   Napoleon I. Youthful bust to left, 1796. Mars seated. Italian cam-
      paign. AE. silvered. Size 40. Holed above head. V. G. Very rare.

345   France. Various small silver medals, different occasions, Louis XVIII.
      Henry IV, Napoleon III, etc. Fine, described. 5 pcs.

346   1795. France. Male figure throwing down an enemy a body at his
      feet, 2 trumpets. Battles of Peschiera and Castiglione. Bell metal.
      Size 43. Fine. Rare.

347   Napoleon I. Emperor seated by a rock. Waar Zal 1k Ontkommen.
      Rev. Bonaparte of St. Helena. AE. Fine.

348   Napoleon I. Various medalets and jetons, different. Mostly Fine. De-
      scribed. 7 pcs.

349   1836. Napoleon I. Bust to r. by Montagny. Arch of Triumph, Fin-
      ished by L. Philippe. Two small rim holed for suspending. Thick AE.
      Size 52 Rare.

350   1741. Papal. Benedict XIV. Bust to right, name. Rev. Reconstruc-
      tion of portico of Liberian Basilica. Building. Below Romulus & Remus
      and wolf. Silver. Size 23. Rare. Original.

351   Milan. Bust of John Galeaza. Rev. Cathedral of Milan. Handsome
      Italian bronze. Size 46. Sharp, uncirculated.

352   Milan. Francis. Bust to 1, 1816. Arms Coronation. Size 42. AE.
      Unc. Handsome workmanship.

353   Another, similar, smaller size. AE. Fine.

354   1837. Milan. Busts of Ferdinand I and Anna. Rev. Virtue seated.
      Marriage Handsome AE. Size 50. Unc.

355   1838. Bust in Iron crown, formerly worn by Napoleon. Coronation
      data. AE. Size 45. VF.

356   1844. Milan. Bust of Ambrosius De Nava, Count of Melita. Rev.
      Monument. Size 46. Handsome AE. Unc. Sharp.

357   1844. Milan. Minerva and Science before tablet. Congress of Science.
      AE. Size 55. Unc. Artistic.

358 1693. Italy. Marcellus, Philosopher. Bust to left, name. Rev. Figure lying on pedestal Tutissimo, Lumine Exhibitio. AE. thick, size 35. Fine portrait and original. Very rare. VF.

359 Milan Charity medal. City standing protecting poor Data. AE. Size 46. Ex. F.

360 1783. Sicily. Bust of Victor Amadeus III to r. Name. Rev. 2 females. Institut. Royal Academy of Science. AE. Size 45. Unc., half red. Original. V. Rare.

361 1847. Sardinia. Bust of Carl Albert. The King. Data. Recognition by people? AE. Size 50. Unc.

362 1662. Piombino. Ruffed bust of Paul Jordan II to r, handsome style. Rev A flor and plant Vultui Suavis Asperi Manui 1622. Ursinorum. AE. Size 56. Cast. V. Fine. Rare. and old.

363 Lombardy. Ferdinand I. Bust. Rev. Coronation scene. 1838. Handsome AE. by Manfredini. Size 52. Rare.

364 Italy. Lupo, Historian. Bust to right. Name. Rev. History, map. VG. AE. 41. Rare.

365 1815. Venice. Italia seated by Lion. 1849. Commemorative of battles with Austria. AE. Size 50. Unc.

366 1866. Water & Street scenes of Venice. Festival to Victor Emanuel II. AE. Size 47. Unc. Rare.

367 Etruria. Genius of Etruria holding torch and flag, near a river god, arms of Austria in field. Rev. Inscription of Unity of Italy. Heavy thick AE. Size 65 .MM. Sharp. Unc. Rare.

368 Costagutus. Bust of Cardinal to r. Rev. City view. Size 40. G. Rare and old.

369 **Papal.** Bust of Christ with halo to left. Door Walled up. Jubilee of Gregory XIV. Original AE. Size 35. Rare.

370 Handsome portrait of Leo XII in papal hat. Rev. Christ with disciples, above this heads of two saints facing; below all, papal keys. Restoration of Bascilica. AE. Size 46. Sharp. Unc. Rare and choice.

371 Gregory XVI. Bust to r. Rev. Nude infants holding cap, keys etc. Basilica of St. John Lateran. AE. Size 44. Unc.

372 —Pius IX. Bust to r. Rev. Ruins of Basilica of St. Paul, burned in 1823. AE. Size 50. Abt. F. Scarce.

373 Bust of Pius IX to 1. Papal hat, keys, by Key. WM. Unc.

374 1609. Tuscany. Bust of Cosimus II, with mantle over armour. Rev. A knot between two hands. A very rare original AE. Size 38. Fine. Rare.

375 1609. Another, different bust to r. Rev. Public Commodity. AE. Size 38. Holed. Good. Original.

376 Dog Medal. Obv. A Collie. The Collie Ass'n. of Penn'a. Wreath. Silver, size 34. V. F. Rare.

377 Phila., Pa. Very large Policeman's brass badge, size 3x3 ½ inches. No| 33. Very rare and old.

378 Wassau, Wis., G. A. R. Md. Expo. Md. Expo., McHenry AE., Exposition 1876, Milwaukee Bay medal, Springfield, Mass, G. A. R. Hon. Frank Brown, Md. Agr. AE. Jamestown Expo, Md. Institute medal. Mostly above 35 MM. Fine. 10 pcs.

379 1865. Abraham Lincoln. Bust r. Names. Rev. Column. WM. Size 50 Ex. F.

380 Geo. Washn. Bust. Rev. View of medal cabinet. Large AE. medal. in plush case. Unc.

381 1876. Centennial, Phila. Large Bronze gilt medal. 3 females. Liberty with sword. Perfect, size 57. Handsome.

382 U. S. Navy. Sharp-shooter's Maltese cross, bar and pin. Fred L. Larson, 7-24-12. Very fine. Rare. First in my sales. Silver.

383 U. S. Navy. Expert Rifleman's badge, two guns crossed, wreath, bar and pin. Ex. Fine. Silver. Rare, First in my sales.

384 Large Chinese Bronze medal, holed center, showing a chinaman, size 55 F.

385 Abraham Lincoln. Bust to r, name, 1809-1865. Rev. "1809-1909. With malice toward none, with charity" etc. Memorial. WM. Size 52. Unc. Scarce.

386 Milan Cathedral. Large bronze gilt medal. Exterior view. Rev. Interior view. Handsome architectural medal. Size 47. Unc. in plush case.

387 Military Buttons. 1776-1864. An interesting collection all different, includes Revolutionary War of 1812. Mostly fine and very rare lot, includes Ireland, with harp, worth up to 50c each. 40 pcs.

388 1817. Rare Martin Luther medal. Box made out of a medal with his bust. Rev. Open book; "And God Said Let There Be Light and There Was Light." etc. The Box contains twelve original hand-painted pictures each depicting an event of Luther's life. Size 38. Unc. Very rare. First in my sales. In original box and frame.

389 France. Marshall MacDonald. Bust to left, name, titles. Rev. List of Appointments. etc. AE. silvered. Size 50. Rare. V. Fine.

390 Military Order of The Serpent. Cross in which a serpent, "Military Order Of The Serpent." With original ribbon. An order of Veterans of The Spanish-American War. Cost $4.00. Unc.

391 International Bi-Metal Dollar. Bust of U. S. Grant. Value in monies of various nations. V. Fine. Rare.

392 1841 53. John Tyler and Franklin Pierce. Rev. Eagle, stars. AE. proofs, by Brichaut. 2 pcs.

393 1834. England. Wm. Till. Rare token, penny size, Numismatist. Rare date. Unc.

394   Cal. Slug token. Obv. of $50 gold. Eagle, banner. "The Days of Old,
      The Days of Gold, The Days of '49". Unc.
394a Rare Washington Token. Head. "George Washington Security." Rev.
      "First in Peace". "First in Preparedness". Silver. Size 30. Unc.
      Very rare.
394b Same, in German Silver. Copper, Brass. Unc. Rare. 3 pcs.
394c Head of A. Lincoln. 1916. "Lincoln Did Not Show the White Feather".
      Rev. Quotation from speech on enforcement of the law. Silver. Rare.
      Size 30.
394d Same in Copper. G. Silver. Brass. Rare. 3 pcs.

(Intermission of twenty minutes)

COLLECTION OF LARGE U. S. CENTS.

Affording An Opportunity For The Collector of Varieties.

394a 1794. Hays 43. Good.
395   1794. Various varieties, including rarities, Poor to fair. 17 pcs.
396   1795. Various, thick and thin flans. Poor to fair. 9 pcs.
397   1796. Various types and numbers. Poor and fair, some rare. 15 pcs.
398   1797. Various. Poor to fair, large number of varieties. 16 pcs.
399   1798 (6), 1800 (6). Fair lot. 12 pcs.
400   1800. Various dies. Avg. Fair. 19 pcs.
401   1800. Good. 2 pcs.
402   1801. Various including errors Avg. Fair. 10 pcs.
402a 1801. Various dies. V. Fair. Scarce. 10 pcs.
403   1802. Various dies, Fair and V. Fair. 20 pcs.
404   1802. Various dies. Fair lot. 30 pcs.
405   1802. 2 var. G and VG. 2 pcs.
406   1803. Small date and 1/100. Abt. Fine.
407   1803. Various dies. V. Fair to good. 17 pcs.
408   1803. Various dies Fair. 25 pcs.
409   1805. Poor to V. Fair (4), 1806 (5). Fair. 9 pcs.
410   1807. Several varieties. Fair. 14 pcs.
411   1807 (6), 1808 (3), 1810 (15), 1812 (15). Fair to good. 39 pcs.
412   1809. Fair. Date good, rare.
413   1809. Fair. Rare. 2 pcs.
414   1809. Poor. Rare. 4 pcs.
415   1811. Perf. date. Very fair, scarce.
416   1811. Over date. Fair; scarce.
417   1811. Poor. 2 pcs.
418   1813. Avg. Fair. 8 pcs.

419 1814. Various dies and varieties fair to good. **21 pcs.**

420 1816 (4), 1817, 15 stars (1) 1819, L. date, 1821 (3). G. & VG. 9 pcs.

421 1818. Unc., red.

422 1824. Close perf. date. Abt. Fine. Rare.

423 1835. Pointed coronet, 1838. Fine. 2 pcs.

423a 1838. Uncirculated, red. Choice example.

424 1839. Silly head. About Unc., brown color.

425 1839. Over 1836. Edge nicks. Very fair. Very rare.

426 1839, over 1836. Very fair. Very rare.

427 1841, 18423. Type '42· Fine. 2 pcs.

428 1843. Type '42· Fine. 2 pcs.

429 1844, over 1881, 1846, double 1. V. Fair. 2 pcs.

430 1844. Double cut. 8 V. Fine.

431 1844, over 1881. Fine. Rare.

432 1845-46, tall 6, also double 1.G to F. 3 pcs.

433 1846. Double 1, double 6, small dates. Fine. 2 pcs.

434 1847. Entire date double struck. VG. Very rare.

435 1847. Perfect date. Uncirculated, brown color.

436 1848. Double struck 1. V. Good, rare.

437 1848. Entire date double struck. Good **Very rare.**

438 1851. over 1881. Good. **Rare.**

439 1851. Unc, red.

440 1851, 1852, 1853. Unc., 2 red. 3 pcs.

441 1853. Unc., bright red.

442 1853. Unc., bright red.

443 1853. Double cut 3. Ex. fine.

444 1853. Unc, bright red, choice. 2 pcs.

445 1853, 1856. Slanting 5 Unc., red. 2 pcs.

446 1857. L. & small dates. V. Fine. 2 pcs.

447 1857. Small date (6). VG. & Fine. 6 pcs.

448 1857. Large date. Mostly fine. 9 pcs.

448a 1858. Eagle Cent. Unc.

U. S. SILVER DOLLARS.

449 1798. Small, close date. Heraldic eagle. V. Good.

450 1798. Wide small date. Heraldic eagle. Very good.

451 1798. Very good, but stamped on obverse.

452 1799. Six stars facing, small stars. V. Good.

453 1799. Six stars facing. Large stars. V. Good.

454 1799. Small star, small date. V. Good.

455 1842. Almost uncirculated.

455a 1855. Very good. **Rare.**
456   Standard Proof dollars, 1879-81-84. 3 pcs.
457   1894. Proof. Smallest No. except 1895.
458   1882. 1900. Various proof. Dollars. 5 pcs.

HALF DOLLARS

459   1805, 1806, 1807. Fair & Good. 4 pcs.
460   1805, 1806. Good. 2 pcs.
461   **1805.** Very good.
462   1823. Ill-formed 3. Uncirculated.
463   1836. Milled. Edge. Almost uncirculated, rare and choice.
464   1839. New Orleans. Mark above date as on rare 1838. Abt. Fine.
465   1860. Proof. Rare.
466   1894, 1906. Proofs. **2 pcs.**

QUARTERS—TWENTY CENTS, ETC.

467   1822, 1825. Very good. 2 pcs.
468   1825. E stamped above head. Ex. fine.
469   1837, 1838, 1840. Fine. VF. & Unc. 3 pcs.
470   1849. About Unc. Rare state.
471   1861, 1863. About Unc. 2 pcs.
472   1892. O. Uncirculated.
473   1893. Isabella. Queen crowned. Unc. Issued at $1.
474   1913. Denver. Unc.
475   1914. Denver. Unc., bright.
476   Twenty Cents. 1875. San Fran. Unc.
477   1875. Carson City. Fine, scarce.
478   1875. Fine.
479   1878. Brill. Proof. Rare. Priced now at $10.
480   Half Dimes. 1841. Unc . Rare.
481   1846. Very good. **Rare.**
482   1872 S. In wrth, 1873. S. F. & V. G. 2pcs.
483   Various half dimes, all different 1831 & later to 1873. Fine and very
      fine. 12 pcs..
484   Three Cents Silver. 1859-61-62. Unc. 3 pcs.
485   1867. Unc. Rare.
486   1870. Unc. Scarce date.
487   1870. Ex. fine, scarce date and Ex. F.
488   Various Uncirculated 3 cts silver. 10 pcs.
489   Three Cents Nichel. 1870. Proof. Rare.
490   1871. Proof. Rare.
491   1872, 1873, 1875, 1876. Proofs all rare. 4 pcs.

492   1878. Proof. V. Rare. None struck for circulation.

493   1879-81 to 1889 inclusive, includes 1887 over 1886. All proofs. Scarce
lot. 10 pcs.

494   Various Proof of 3c Nickels, in '80s' rare (10) Unc. (12). 22 pcs.

495   **Two Cents Bronze.** Uncirculated lot, some red. Dups. 20 pcs.

496   Uncirculated 2 cts, dups. Some red. 22 pcs.

CHOICE FOREIGN COPPER COINS.

Including Many Rare and Interesting.

497   Goa. Thick 15 and 30½ Reis. Good. Rare and old. 2 pcs.

498   1860. Goa. ½ Macuta. Large. Unc., rare state.

499   Spain. Philip IV. Busts. 8 and 16 M. Fine. 3 sizes. 3 pcs.

500   Barbadoes. Moses Tolanto farthing. Barrel. About Unc. Very rare
this size. First in my sales.

501   Jamaica. Edw. VII and Victoria. All diff. ¼ to 1 D. Unc. 4 pcs.

502   British N. Borneo. Wild Men. Cent. Proof Red.

503   1824. Nova Scotia. Head of Geo. IV Thistle. Penny. Extremely
fine. Scarce condition.

504   1797. Coventry Half Penny. Elephant arms. White Friars Gate.
Proof. Rare.

505   1797. Coventry Half Penny. Rev. View of White Friars Building
Proof.

506   1797. Coventry Half Penny. View of St. Mary Hall. Red proof.
Rare.

507   1797. Coventry Half Penny. View of Mill Lane Gate. Proof. Rare.

508   1791. St. Bevois Southampton Half Penny. Head. Rev. Shield.
Proof Rare.

509   1770. Tay Bridge Half Penny. Man gathering fish out of a seine.
Proof. Rare.

510   John Thelwall Half Penny. Bust to r. Rev. Radiate liberty cap LIB-
ERTAS 1796. Red proof. Rare.

511   1796. Royal plumes. Rev. Fame with trumpet Public Half Penny.
Proof.

512   1791. Sierra Leone. One Penny. Dull proof.

513   1794. British India. Bale mark. 1/96 R. Daler. Proof.

514   197. Coventry Half Penny. Arms. Rev. View of Spon Gate. Proof.

515   1794. Coventry. Godiva Half Penny. Steeple. Fine.

516   1762. Bohemia. Maria Theresa. Bust. kreuzer. Fine.

517   1852. Baden. Bust of Leopold. 1 Kr., Unc., red.

518   1816. Austria. Arms. Ein Kreuzer. Unc, red. Rare state.

519   1629. Malta. John Paul Lascaris Castellar. Broad 4 Tari. Cstpd by various Nights of Malta. Fine. Rare. (Scott $2).

520   As last, but 2 Tari, Emanuel De Rohan. St. John's head, 1786-96. Clasped hands XX,X and V Tari. Good. 4 pcs.

521   Sweden. Gustavus Adolphus. Agriffin walking to left. Arms. Broadl Or. Fine for this crude piece. Rare and in great demand.

522   1627. Sweden. Nykoping. Broad viece. Eagle with outspread wings. Arms. Good. Very rare. 1 Or.

523   1686. Sweden. 3 Crowns. Griffin. 1/6 Or Fine.

524   1796. Luxemburg. Thick siege 1 Sol, cast, bell metal. Fine. Rare.

525   1797. Papal Pius VI. Severino. ½ Bai. Fine.

526   1789. Russia. Cath II. ¼ Kop. Unc.

527   1844. Russia. Thick 2 Kopeks. Unc., half red.

528   1867-75. Finland. 1 5 and 10 Penni. Unc., red. 3 pcs.

529   1841. Russia. 1 Kopek. Unc., red.

530   1869. Brazil. Dom Pedro. Bust. 20 R. Unc. red.

531   1821. Brazil. XX Reis. Unc., half red.

532   1840. Buenos Ayres. 1 Real. Unc., red almost Pf.

533   1848. England. Victoria Model. V. Fine.

534   1728. Russia. Peter II. Kopek. VG.

535   Wismar, Corvey, Cosvelt 3 to 7 Pfg. F. 3 pcs.

536   Isle of Man. Victoria ¼ & I D. G. & V. G. 2 pcs.

537   1774. Siberia. Sables supporting shield. Monogram of Catherine II. Heavy. broad 10 Kepeks. Very fine. Value $2.50.

538   1660. Riga. Bust of John Casimir. Rev. Same mounted. Solidus. Fine.

539   1841-58. Jersey. Victoria 1-13. 1-26 and 1-52 Shilling. Unc, red. 3 pcs.

540   1858. Jersey, 1-26 Shill; 1866-44., 1-13, 1-24 and 1-48 Shill. Unc., red. 4 pcs.

541   1909. Jersey. Edw. VII. Bust 1-12 and 1-24 Sill. Unc., red. 2 pcs.

542   1861. Jersey. Victoria. Large 1-13 Shill. Unc. Scarce.

BROKEN BANK BILLS, ETC.

543   New York. "Fifty Cent Note. 1858. Indian. V. G. Rare.

544   1808. Gloucester, RI. Old bills for $5, $10. Fine examples of earliest American Bk Notes. 2 pcs.

545   1837. Republic of Texas. $100. Cancelled. Very rare.

546   1837. Deer Creek, Md. notes, 6½ & $1. V. F. 3 pcs.

547   Fine Collection of all different Broken Bank notes, includes some choice Northern Banks. Many fine and Unc. 36 pcs.

548 $1,000. Anti Greenback money. Ben Butler. "The Mint". Rev. Man Feeding geese; $1,000 Phoenix Mutual Ins. Co., 1790. R. L. Lottery ticket; Parish D'Iberville 50c Note, La.; Drakes Plantation Bitters $100. Mostly F. Scarce. 6 pcs.

549 C. S. A. Sept. 10, 1861. $50. Washu. Two females in center. Note B3808. Crisp. So. Bk Notes Co. Value $4.00.

550 Nov. 20, 1862. $100. Negroes. X Blocked letters, watermarked. Unc. Rare.

551 Aug. 26, 1862. $100 Cars. Letter Z. Note 1511. Crisp. Bradbeer 320 Rarity A. Mr. Bradbeer states he never saw another.

552 Oct. 29, 1862. $100. Negroes hoeing Cotton. W. Crisp. Rare.

553 Dec. 18, 1862. $100 Negroes. Y. & Z. Unc. 2 pcs.

554 Sutler's Money, Civil War. 3 diff. Scotts and Mass Regt. Unc. 3 pcs.

554a 1861. C. S. A. $100. Cars. So. Bk. Note Co. B 4070. Very fine. Cancelled. None missing. Very rare.

CONSIGNMENT OF PISTOLS, WEAPONS AND CURIOS

Part I

555 6 Shot Under Ring Trigger Pepper Box, Elliott's Patent. Good. Very rare.

556 Sharps Pepper Box 4 shot, 22. Low number, 375. Almost new. Rare state.

557 Sharps 4 shot, 32 Cal. Pepper Box, elaborately engraved. No. 14975. V. Fine.

558 Sharp's Pepper Box. 22 Cal. Side Button Ejector. Wooden handle. Good. Very rare.

559 Rare Colt. Half Fluted Cylinder, 36 Cal. 36½ inch barrel, the barrel round, engraved and gold-plated. Ivory Handled. In fine state and very rare.

560 5 Shot 31 calibre Remington Percussion Pistol. Rare type with the nipple sunk in cylinder Fine. Valuable.

561 Five shot 31 Calibre, Beal's Patent Remington. Rare. Trigger does not work. Can easily be fixed, otherwise very good.

562 Five shot, 34. (?), or 36 Cal. Remington, 1858, New Model Ilion, NY. 4 inch barrel. In fine state, and said to be a very rare type.

563 Five Shot Ring Trigger Remington small Pepper Box pistol, 22 cal. Very good order, and rare. Elliott's Patent.

564 Heavy Signal Pistol, with ¾ inch bore Robertson. Only fair state. Rare.

565 Single shot, ½ Octagon and half round barrel, G. S. P. stamped on barrel. Scarce. V. Good.

566   6 shot 38 Calibre. Nat'l Arms Co. Brooklyn Very good condition.

567   Six shot 32 Cal "Peace Maker" Pistol. Fair state.

568   Old cap and ball pistol.

569   Curious "Knuckle Duster," Pistol, "My friend." 2 Cal. Rare. Very good.

570   Silver mounted, Ivory handled Italian dagger, with solid silver sheath. Rare and fine, has silver guard.

571   Heavy I. X. L. Wostenholm Hunter's Knife, with handsome horn handle and German silver and leather sheath, size 12½ inches, blade dimensions 2x8 inches. Valuable and fine.

572   Combination Saw and Knife. As new. Length 9 inches.

573   Odd 22 Calibre Single Shot Remington, flat hammer Pistol, which strikes on head of cartridge. Rare.

574   Liquid Pistol, for shooting water, acids, etc., also a make-believe pistol. 2 pcs.

575   Large Revolutionary War Powder horn. Cow's Horn, with leather sling, and lead powder measure attached. Fine and rare, bears name of owner, M. Buzby.

576   Peacroft Sheffield sharp tapering point knife, the blade engraved with defiant eagle and "We ask for nothing but what is right and Submit to nothing that is wrong," with ornamented German silver handle and sheath. Fine length over all 11 inches.

577   Old Italian Ivory handled stiletto, silver tipped. Length of blade 7¾ inches. Rare, in brass sheath.

578   U. S. Army Regulation Ice Knife or pick, with four prongs, as new, length 10 inches.

579   Ancient Roman Pottery Lamp, Ornamented with arrow head design. 4 x1½ inches. Second Century AD. From catacombs. Used by early Christians.

580   A Second Clay Lamp in fine state.

581   A third Roman Catacombs Lamp, differing from preceding, mouth mended.

582   Boatman's Silver Whistle, size 1x5½ inches.

583   Fossil Shark's Tooth, two alligator teeth and 2 Beaber Teeth. 5 pcs.

584   Babylonian Clay Tablet, B. C. 2350. Last kings of Ur. Inscribed with cuneiform writing. Fine and interesting.

585   Another tablet, just as old and fine.

586   Miniature Holy Bible, 11/4x1¾ inches. 700 pp. Imported. New.

587   Miniature Khaki covered Bible "Allies", with Kipling's Recessional, 700 pp. Very unusual.

588   Miniature New Testament, ¾ size of U. S. 2c stamp, perfectly printed on fine paper, over 400 pages. Imported. As new.

589   Babylonian Stone Cylinder Seal, before 2500 B. C.   Used to roll over the clay tablets, and kept by priests. Rare.

590   OLD PISTOLS. Cowles & Son, Chicopee, Mass., single shot, center fire, 3½ inch barrel. Very good. Worth $25 to $30.

591   Rare Six shot, Cal. Under-hammer Pepper Box, no name, possibly Elliott's make, very thick barrel, size 3x1-1; 2 inches. Good order and very rare.

592   Six Shot English Pistol, possibly Adams. Fine order, 38 Cal.

593   New York 31 Cal. Colt, five shot 32. Very good.

594   Hopkins & Allen 32 Cal. 5 shot, yellow amber or celluloid handles, nickel plated Good.

595   Three various old pistols, different. Very fair. 3 pcs.

596   Ethan Allen center fire, very small, single shot, 2 inch barrel Good. Rare.

597   Turkish Flint-Lock, about 50 yrs old, 8 inch barrel. Needs repairs. Fair.

598   Turkish Flint-Lock. 150 yrs old, 7 inch barrel, fancy ornamented butt Good state, with flint.

599   Old Turkish Flint-Lock, brass mounted Pistol, 150 yrs old, 13 inch barrel. Good.

600   Single Shot, Cap and ball centre hammer, 3½ inch barrel. Very fair.

601   Cap and ball, single shot, center hammer, 22 Poor. 2 pcs.

602   Long dagger from cane, mounted, length 16 inches.

603   Double edged Cutlass blade length 14 inches, in sheath, brass handle.

604   Heavy U. S. Navy Cutlass, heavy brass hilt, dated 1862. Fine.

605   Long foreign sword or cutlass, an old weapon, length of blade 19 inches

606   Large antique hand made knife, or dagger, very odd. 1.12 in.

607   Large old Trowel Bayonet, scarce.

608   Three fine Powder measures, one leather, all brass mounted. 3 pcs.

609   Odd large wooden pipe, "Sea Monster" and Indian Pappoose ornament. 4 pcs.

610   Two Small Powder Flasks, pewter and brass. 2 pcs.

611   Four all different powder flasks, all diff. leather, pewter, etc. Good lot. 4 pcs.

612   Fine Metal powder flask, length 7½ inches.

613   Revolutionary Powder Horn. (Cow horn), engraving of a ship. Fine condition.

614   Very fine Revolutionary War Powder Horn. Very clean surface in perfect condition. Best I have offered for condition.

615 Arizona Indian clay pipe bowl.

616 Old Octagon Barrel Pistol, Cap and ball, side hammer style, length of barrel 3½ inch. Very good. Rare.

617 Small, very old Powder flask, design, eagle, shield, E. PLURIBUS UNUM.

618 Indian horse-hair dyed various colors bead string with Catlinite pendant. Rare and fine.

619 Heavy Starr Arms Co. NY. 44 Pistol. 5½ inch barrel.

620 Marston & Knox 6 shot 32 pepper box. Fair, could be improved. Rare.

621 Colts, NY. 31 Cal 5 shot pistol. Repair to spring needed otherwise V. Good.

622 Heavy British Constabulary Pistol, bull dog type 44 Cal. Good.

623 Lafechaux Pistol, stock damaged, works OK. 32 Cal.

624 Five Old Powder Pouches and measures, 3 leather. 5 pcs.

625 Pair of very heavy wooden shoes, with sharp-pointed toes. 2 pcs.

626 Indian brass bell. Diameter 4 in, holder broken at top.

627 Ancient Roman Pottery vase, height 4½ inches. Good.

628 A. D. 300. Roman gracefully modeled Glass Bottle with wide body and narrow mouth, size 4x5½ inches. Perfect and rare.

629 A. D. 300. Gracefully modeled Roman glass bottle, size 4x5 inches. Perfect and rare.

630 A. D. 300. Long Roman glass bottle, size 6x3 inches. Perfect and rare.

631 Three beautifully modeled Roman Glass bottles, two chipped at top, one has small hole in body, also 5 fragments of Roman glass. 8 pcs.

For Additional Pistols, Weapons, etc. See Lots 760-768 inclusive.

632 Section of vertebrae of a Fossil Shark. Phosphite beds of S. Car. Said to be from 3 to 5,000,000 years old.

633 Fine Fossil Shark's Tooth, hard black, glossy petrification, size 2¼x 1¼ inches. S. Car Phosphite beds. Rare.

634 Another Fossil Shark's Tooth, larger size 3x2 inches. Good. Rare.

635 Six Fossil Shark's Teeth, of various sizes up to 1½ inch. Black and brown colors. Phosphite Beds. S. Car. 5 pcs.

ANCIENT COINS.

636 GOLD. Rome. Valentinian II. Head r. Two seated, VICTORIA AVG. G. C. O. II. Treves Mint. Solidus. Fine.

637 Greece. Peloponessus, Antigoneia, Achean Tetrobols G. 2 pcs.

638 (B. C. 400). Sicyon. Tetrobol; B. C. 468. Argos. Triobol VG. 2 pcs.

639 (B. C. 400). Istrus. Persian stater. Two heads joined; Larissa, B. C. 400, stater; Pharcadon, Thessaly. Man restraining bull. Triobol. Holed. V. Good. 3 pcs.

640 (B. C. 480). Thessaly. Pharsalus Triobol (holed), Phocis, (B. C. 357). Tribol G. first holed. 2 pcs.

641 (B. C. 357). Phocis. Head of bull. Triobol. VG. Rare.

648 (B. C. 313). Euboea. Histiaea. Head, prow. Tribols. G. 2 pcs.

649 (B. C. 280). Illyria. Dyrrachium. Thrace. Triobols. G. 2 pcs.

650 (B. C. 480). Chersonseus. Forepart of lion, turning back Triobol, Cardia mint. VG.

651 (B. C. 400). Euboea. Chalcis. Tetrobol and drachm. Both holed. Chersonseus, Triobol, all holed, G. & VG. 3 pcs.

652 (B. C. 411). Macedon. Neapolis. Grinning mask. Head. Triobol. VG.

653 (B. C. 400). Thrace Byzantium. Bull. Rev. Punch-mark. Persic drachm. G. Rare.

654 Macedonia. Alexander I. Triobol; Neapolis, Triobol, (holed). Fair. 2 pcs.

655 Macedon. Alexander III. Drachm. s. Fair. 2 pcs.

656 (B. C. 500). Thasos. Satyr, nymph. Punchmark. Drachm. Good Rare.

657 Parthia, B. C. 136, Phraates II, drachm (holed); Cappadocia, Ariobarzanes I and III Drachms. VG. 3 pcs.

658 Macedonia. Alexander III Drachms. Fair. 2 pcs.

659 (B. C. 200). Rhodes. Drachm Head. Flower. Good.

660 (B. C. 300). Corinth. Tetrobol. Head. Pegasus. VG.

661 (B. C. 400). Head. Flower. Stater, VG.

662 (B. C. 400). Sinope. Head. Eagle, fish. Drachm. Test cut, VG. Rare.

663 (B. C. 500). Athens. Head of Pallas, large size. Owl. Tetradrachm. Good. Rev. V. Good.

664 (B. C. 450). Cholcis. Nymph. Bull. Triobols. G. 2 pcs.

665 ROME. (B. C. 44). Julius Caesar. Head. Aeneas and Anchises. Denarious. V. Fine.

666 Caesar. Elephant. CAESAR. Boutificial implements. Denarius. V. Fine.

667 Augustus. Head. Two Caesars. Denarius. Fine.

668 Faustina I. Bust Ceres. Denarius. Fine.

669 Tiberius. Head. Livia seated. Tribute penny. Attempted punc_ture. Fine.

670 Panonia. Tetradrachms. Barbaric style after those of Philip II of Cacedon. Fine. Rare.

671 Syria. Flavius Vespasian. Broad tetradrachm, found in Syria. Head Eagle. G. to V. G. Rare. Good silver.

672   Tiberius.   Head.   Hippopotamus.   Small bronze.   Fine.   Rare.

673   Trajan. Colonial Tetr.   Head eagle, open wings.   holed near bottom.
      Fine, very good silver.

674   Various Small bronzes.   Greek & Roman Poor & Fair.   7 pcs.

675   **Judea.**   Head of Vespasian.   Rev. Judea under tree.   Denarius.   Good.
      Rare.

676   John Hyrcanus Mites.   Good.   2 pcs.

677   Herod the Great.   Cornucopia.   Anchor.   Mite.   Fine and rare.

678   Another, similar.   Mite.   Very good.   Rare.

679   Archelaus.   Poppy head.   Leaf.   Mite.   Very good.   Very rare.

680   Nero.   Mite.   Vase.   Grapes.   Mite.   Very good.   Very rare.

681   Agrippa, appointed, by Caligula.   Year VI Mite.   Fine for coin.   Rare.

682   Bar Vochab.   Sixth Shekel.   Palm Tree, Grape lead.   **Without the
      year.**   Very rare.   Very fair.

683   Bar-Cochab.   Sixth Shekel.   Palm Tree.   Grape Leaf.   Without The
      Year.   Abt. Fine.   **Very rare.**

684   Bar-Cochab.   Smaller coins.   Vase Leaf.   V. Good.   Very rare.

685   Another.   Very fine.   Rare.

686   **Miscellaneous Ancient Coins.**   (B. C. 400).   Metapontum.   Head of
      Leukippos. in helmet.   Rev.   Wheat Ear.   Stater.   Good.   Rare.

687   Macedon.   Alexander III.   Hercules.   Zeus.   Drachm.   VG.

 688   Rome.   Allectus Head.   R. Rev Pax AUG. ML.   3rd Bronze.   Fine.
      Rare.

689   Another, Allectus.   Smaller head.   Galley with rowers.   VIRTVS AVG.
      3rd bronze.   Fine.   Rare.

690   (A. D. 518).   Byzantium.   Head of Justinus I.   Head.   Emperor
      standing.   Denarius.   V. G.   Very rare.

691   Justinus I.   Bust to r.   I B.   Thick small bronze coin, issued at Alex-
      andria Fine and rare.

692   Trajan.   Broad 1st bronze.   Bust.   Rev. Nile reclining.   Cast.   Very
      good. rare.

693   (B. C. 280).   Velia.   Pallas head, in helmet.   Rev. Lion devouring a
      stag.   Stater.   Very good.   Rare type.

694   Rome.   Lot of Various denarii, mostly later billon type.   Average
      good.   33 pcs.

Two Interesting Hunter's Outfits.

695   Old-Time Squirrel Hunter's Bullet Pouch of deer-skin, with Powder
      Horn attached.   Good, and a rare combination.   1 lot.

696   Very old Powder Horn with leather bullet pouch attached.   Secured
      from an old Indian Chief in New Mexico.   Has cartridge measure at-
      tached.   All good state.   1 lot.

697 1908. Small Cents, S. Mint, Indian head. V. Fine. Scarce. 50 pcs.

698 1909. S. Mint. Indian head cents. V. Fine. Rarest of all later date cents. 25 pcs.

699 1909. S. Mint. Lincoln cents, with V. D. B. V. Fine. Rare. 25 pcs.

700 1864. $2.00. C. S. A. Benjamin Notes. Crips notes, A to H inclusive. Scarce lot. 8 pcs.

701 1864. C. S. A. $2. As last, A to H incl. All but 2 unc. 8 pcs.

702 Old Military Buttons, 1812 war and later, all different, some large. 12 pcs.

703 Miniature New Testament, ¾ size of postage stamp, beautifully printed. Imported. Over 400 pages. As new.

704 Babylonian Clay Tablets, 2350 B. C. Perfect and inscribed.

705 Egyptian Scarab, before 1500 B. C. Inscribed and in fine state.

706 Ancient beads, Egyptian Roman and Greek (50). Wampum, various, some old, (50), Mound Builders disc pottery money (10). Interesting. 110 pcs.

707 Large lot foreign copper and nickel coins and tokens, all conditions up to uncirculated. 500 pcs.

708 Large U. S. Cents, date before 1815. Poor and fair. 50 pcs.

709 U. S. Cent Collection, all different dates or varieties, including some before 1815. 45 pcs.

710 U. S. Half Cents, poor, and fair. The most collected U. S. Coins. 35 pcs.

711 Another lot of U. S. Half Cents, poor or fair. 35 pcs.

712 U. S. Dimes, old types before 1838. Good. 20 pcs.

713 Old U. S. Three Cts. Nickel. Good to fine. Good assortment of dates. 100 pcs.

714 U. S. Two Cents bronze, good assortment of dates. Good. 100 pcs.

715 U. S. 3 Cts. Silver. Fair average, some good. 40 pcs.

716 Curious Collection. A Jeweler's Scrap Heap. Includes thousands of watch wheels and pieces, chains, keys, screws, bolts, entire works of antique watches and various odd pieces of jewelry, and fragments, with some small pieces of gold; also 10 whole watches. In all probably 25,000 pieces. Sold as 1 lot.

717 A collection of 20 very odd antique watch-chains, some of extra size, various materials, mostly new. 20 pcs.

718 Collection of Gems, real and imitation. About 500 pcs. Sold as 1 lot.

719 Varied lot of Pottery, Indian and Oriental China, Curios, etc., an odd assortment, some very good. 30 pcs.

720 Another lot of Pottery, Curios, Antiques, etc., of various kinds, differ- ing from last lot.

LOT OF C. S. A. PAPER MONEY, ETC.

721   C. S. A. Sept. 2, '61· $50 Chest. A-d. Reverse stamped Pay Mobile Savings Bank. V.F. Rare.

722   Sept. 2-61· $100. Wagon. Richmond Va. note. A-g. Abt. F.

723   Dec. 2-62. $100. Mrs. Davis, B. Greenback. Unc. Rare.

724   Apr. 6-13. $50. X-A. VF. Rare.

725   Sept. 25-62. $100. Negroes hoeing cotton. Script watermarked paper. Unc. Rare. Rev. has printing.

726   Feb. 17-64. $500 Jackson. B. & C. Remarkably low numbers, 13640-4012. Fine. Rare. 2 pcs.

727   Feb. 17-64. $500. B. 2020. Ex. F. Remarkably low number. Rare.

728   Feb. 17-64. $500. D-16684. Fine.

729   Feb 17-64. $100. Mrs. Davis. A-B-C-D. VF. 4 pcs.

730   Feb. 17-64. $100. C-2372. Remarkably low No. Fine.

731   Feb. 17-64. $10 C-1808. Unc. Rare. Remarkably low No.

732   $10 F6287-6288, Unc. Low Nos. 2 pcs.

733   Feb. 17-64. $10 G2617. Unc. Low No.

734   Feb. 17-64. $10 A to H incl. V. & VG. 8 pcs.

735   Feb. 17-64· $5.00. **E. Note 41.** A great rarity. To illustrate the rarity, I found many notes numbered over 100,000 in same lot. V. Fair.

736   Feb. 17-64. $5.00. C-381. Several holes. Very rare.

737   Feb. 17-64. $5. A-596 VF. Very rare early Number.

738   Feb. 17-64. $5. B-1801. VF. Rare early No.

739   Feb. 17-64. $5.00. C-853. VG. Very rare early No.

740   Apr. 1863. $10. F-G(2). Stamped on face FEBRUARY 1864. Unc. Rare. 3 pcs.

741   Apr. 1863, $10 G(2). Stamped in red ink, NOVEMBER 1863. F. 2 pcs.

742   Apr. 6, 63. $5 C-F-H. Stamped APRIL, MAY, SEPTEMBER 1863 in red ink on obv. F. 3 pcs.

743   Dec. 2, 1862. $10 Pink. F-Apr. 63. $10. Stamped MAY 1863. VG. 2 pcs.

744   1862. $5. Virginia Treasy. Green. A to D incl. VG. to F. 17 pcs.

745   1862-4. Georgia. $2, $3, 4, $5, $10, $20, $50, Female, temple. Unc. 8 pcs.

746   Ga. Jan. 15-62. $100. A Unc.

747   Ga. Apr. 6, 1864, $100. Female, temple Library. A. Ex. F.

748   Feb. 3-63. Ga. $100. Temple of Liberty only. A. Unc.

749   Jan. 15, 1865. $50. Female standing Note A-76! Unc. Ex. Rare. Low No. and rare year.

750   July 21-62. $1. Va. Treasury Notes, red & black A to D incl. Unc. 10 pcs.

751   Mar. 9-65. Six Per Cent Non Taxable Certificates of C. S. A. for $500. Signed by the Confederate Register of the Treasury. 5 pcs.

752 Oct. 1-61. $5. The Mechs Bk, Augusta. Note No. 90. Signed and issued. VF. Rare.

753 1863. N. Car. 5 cts. A 42, B 42, C 42, D 119, E 42, O 45, P 45, Q 45, R 44, S 44, T 41, U 41. All low Nos. and Unc. 12 pcs.

754 1863. N. Car. 25 cts. A to O inclusive. All 852 or 862. 6 pcs. Unc.

755 1863. N. Car. 50c ship. A to O inclusive, numbers all 65. Unc. 15 pcs.

756 July 26-61. CSA. $20. Ship. C-c. & D., first very thick paper. VG. 3 pcs.

757 Sept. 2-61. $20 Ship A-A and A-5., former No. 1085. Rare. Fine. 2 pcs.

758 1853. $100. Mechs. Bank, Georgia. Note 61. Ancient train of cars. $50 same bank. Very fair. 1 good. Rare. 2 pcs.

759 CSA. Feb. 17-64. $2. Judah P. Benjamin, A to H incl. Crisp. 7 pcs.

COLLECTION OF RARE PISTOLS, WEAPONS, ETC.

PART II.

760 Pair of English ten inch S. H. Martin Percussion pistols. German silver. mounted. Oct. barrels. Cap boxes in stocks. Very fine and rare. 2 pcs.

761 Very early French 15 inch Flint Lock Pistol. Silver head of one of early French Kings Inlaid in butt, Barrels, locks, etc. Beautifully inlaid in barrel, hand chased, etc. Fine working order. Rare.

762 Antique Persian Brass Mounted Rat-tail. Flint lock Pistol. 22 inches long. Good order.

763 French 13 inch half octagon half round barrel pistol, altered to percussion. Beautifully inlaid barrel and stock. Very fair.

764 Large 10 inch Eagle Arms Co., New York, 6 shot, 44 cal. pistol. Rosewood handles. Very fine order. Scarce.

765 Five Shot Allen & Wheelock 8½ inch pistol (percussion), flat hammer and long cylinder. Trigger spring broken. Otherwise very good. Rare.

766 Sharp & Hankins, 32 Cal. 4 shot, pepper-box, side button ejector. Very fine.

767 Six shot Allen & Thurber pepper-box, ivory handle, German silver rim around nipples. Good working order.

768 Five shot 36 Cal. Fluted Cylinder, 11½ inch, round barrel, New York Colt Pistol. Spring does not work, otherwise good. Scarce.

769 Six inch, five shot, Pepper-Box Pistol (no name, probably unique). Very good.

770 Superposed Barrel, 44 Cal. Remington Derringer Pistol. Very good.

771 5 shot, 22 Cal. Ring Trigger Remington Pistol, Perfect order. Factory blueing. Rare.

772 5 shot, 32 Cal., Smith & Wesson, single action, nickle plated Pistol. Perfect order.

773   Single barrel 10 inch Percussion Tenton Pistol (English), German silver mounted. Fair.

774   Five shot, 31 Cal. 8½ inch E. Whitney, New Haven, Pistol, working order. Very good. Scarce.

775   Remington 5 shot 31 Cal. odd cylinder 6½ inch. Gutta percha handles. (loaded, 5 cylinders). Scarce type of Remington.

776   Small 22 Cal. single shot, Remington. Very scarce. Very old pattern. Fine.

777   5 shot Remington Pistol, 22 Cal., Ring Trigger, minus handles and slightly inoperative. Can be fixed up.

778   8 shot Rupertus Pepper-Box Pistol. Side disc and end pin missing. A good piece can be made of this. Very rare.

779   Pair of 11 inch early French Flint lock Pistols. Butt, side-plates, Trigger guard inlaid in silver, with head of Early French King. End of stock on one broken and lock loose on other, otherwise very good. Very rare pair. 2 pcs.

780   Three very early small horn powder horns. Very fine examples. 3 pcs.

781   Early French Dagger, with belt hook on side of sheath—Handle, guard and sheath is engraved and embossed silver, beautifully ornamented in flowers and coils. Very heavy silver and very rare. Finest I have offered.

782   Very old and large Scotch Horn Powder-horn (18 inches long), beautifully carved and polished. Mounted in large silver shield, name plate in silver, with name "I. A. Falcone". Each end "Scotch Carin Gorm" mounted. Rare and fine.

783   Two old wooden Watchmen's Rattles. Very hard, polished wood, one brassbound ("122").

784   9 inch steel turned small cannon, ¾ inch bore. Strong weapon. Fine Condition..

784a   Two other small cannon's different bores and 1 small brass cannon.

785   J. T. Thomas' Patent (Feb 9, 1858) Remington & Sons Ilion, N. Y. Steel Cane Gun. In new condition. Perfect. Very rare and valuable.

786   Single barrel and shot, large bore percussion, Low number 162, pistol. Either Rupertus or Bacon, (no name) 6½ inches, nipple in center of octagonal frame. Very fine condition, rare.

THE END.

Priced Catalogue of The Jackson Tokens.

Offered in this sale, each lot neatly priced in ink, may be obtained on receipt of 25 cts. A valuable record for future reference.

THOMAS L. ELDER

BID BY THE PIECE.

Put Your Name and Address on this Bid Sheet without fail.

--19----

Thomas L. Elder,
  · 32 E. 23rd St., New York City.

        Please execute the following bids at your sale

of ------------------------------------

The Bids are made by the PIECE.

    My bids are so much for each piece.

              Yours truly,

LOT	BID	LOT	BID	LOT	BID

Be sure and place your address on this sheet

(over)

LOT	BID	LOT	BID	LOT	BID

PSIA information can be obtained
www.ICGtesting.com
nted in the USA
HW052356171218
5856BV00020B/936/P